The Official Cat Dictionary

by RICK DETORIE

WALLABY

A WALLABY BOOK
Published by Simon & Schuster
NEW YORK

To Terry, Sandy,
Richie and Mom.

Copyright © 1982 by Rick Detorie

All rights reserved
including the right of reproduction
in whole or in part in any form
Published by Wallaby Books
A Simon & Schuster Division of
Gulf & Western Corporation
Simon & Schuster Building
1230 Avenue of the Americas
New York, New York 10020

WALLABY and colophon are registered
trademarks of Simon & Schuster

First Wallaby Books printing September 1982
10 9 8 7 6 5 4 3 2 1
Manufactured in the United States of America

Printed and bound by Halliday Lithograph

ISBN: 0-671-45624-5

catacombs

catalogging

catalytic converter

catalyze

catamaran

catamount

catamountain

catapult

cataract

catarrh

catastrophe

catatonics

catbird

cat boxes

cat burglar

cat call

catchall

catch-as-catch-can

catch at

catcher

catch in

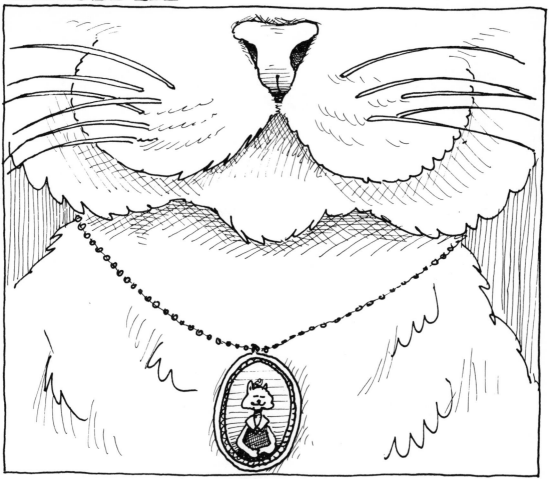

catching

catchment

catechesis

catechism

catechu

categorized

category

catenary

catenate

catering

caterpillar

caterwauling

catfishing

catguts

catharpin

Cathars

cathartic

cathedral

catheter

cathexis

cathode

catholic

catholicity

catkin

catlike

catnip

cat·o·nine·tails

CAT scan

cat's cradle

Catskills

cat's pajamas

cat's paw

catsup

cattail

catty

catty-corner

CATV

catwalk